Cherokee Clans

Cherokee Clans
An Informal History

Donald N. Panther-Yates

Panther's Lodge
Phoenix
2013

On the cover: Paint Clan mask, carved from buckeye wood, hardened with fire, painted with organic and mineral paints and covered with bee's-wax by Virgil Crowe, who single-handedly revived the Cherokee Paint Clan way of making masks. Crowe made this mask as a demonstration of his mask-making art in 1990, Cherokee, North Carolina. The divided colors represent the choice of a warrior or one confronted by a warrior between life (red, the color of the Paint Clan) and death (black). Red and black can also be interpreted as the colors of the East (the source of life) and West (place where the ancestors live, Elohi), as well as the colors of the two paint clans, Ani-Wodi and Ani-Sahoni. *Collection of Donald N. Yates.*

Cherokee Clans: An Informal History © 2013 Donald N. Yates
ISBN-13: 978-0615798271
ISBN-10: 0615798276
Published by Panther's Lodge
Cherokee Chapbooks Series
Expanded Print Edition
Printed in the United States of America
All Rights Reserved.

Orders: 1-888-806-2588 Extension 5
Visit us online at www.pantherslodge.com

If we were naively to pose the question who the Cherokee really are, and what constitute their origins and divisions, we would be forced to admit that anything like definitive accounts are utterly lacking. This is the case even though Cherokees make up one of the oldest—and today most numerous—American Indian groups. Scholars regard them as a sort of enigma. The following notes are offered only in the spirit of sketching some rudimentary facts I personally have been able to piece them together. They are not intended to be anything more than tentative.

The Cherokee clans were suppressed by the reforms of affluent half-breed planters following the death of Dragging Canoe in 1792 and white settlement of Tennessee. The Light Horse Brigade introduced by Maj. Ridge (al-Wadi) was modeled on the prevailing Arab institution of the *qadi*. Henceforth, Cherokee marshals, not clans, had the power to punish acts like illicit sexual intercourse, theft, drunkenness and murder.

The formal decree abolishing clan law was called the Act of Oblivion and signed by Turtle at Home as Speaker, Black Fox as Principal Chief and seconded by Pathkiller and Toochaler, Broomtown, September 11, 1808. A later act was executed at Eustanala, April 18, 1810, "by order of the seven clans."

A conservative Ghost Dance Movement flared up in 1811 when Chief Black Fox died, but by the time of removal to Indian Territory in 1838 clans were little more than a name and a memory. Government rolls ignored them. Even though marriage with someone of your own clan was formerly punishable by death, clan traditions rapidly began to fade. Probably few Cherokee today can recount the clan history of their parents and forebears with any great confidence. Descendants with little Cherokee blood, even those who may preserve a direct female line, are often completely in the dark about clan affiliations.

The Cherokee Seven Clans are unique, distinctive, and unusual. They are Wolf (Ani-Wahiya), Bird (Ani-Tsiskwa), Deer (Ani-Kawi), Twister (Ani-Gilohi),

2

Wild Potato (Ani-Gotegewi), Panther (Ani-Sahoni) and Paint (Ani-Wodi). Before they were codified into seven, considered a sacred number by the Cherokee, there existed clans named raccoon, wildcat, fox, corn, water, Shawnee, crystal, wind, man, tree, tufted titmouse, raven, redbird, bluebird, holly, long prairie, blue, sun, fire, acorn and many, many others. They are not exactly paralleled in other tribes. The Lenape, for instance, have four main clans—Wolf, Turtle, Turkey and Fish. Other Indian peoples are divided into eight—Buffalo, Thunderbird, Turtle, Wolf, Deer, Bird, Otter, and Bear.

Although sometimes combined with the Panther Clan, the Bear Clan is usually ignored in the scheme. Thus Bear Clan members are not assigned a tier of seats in the national heptagon. Traditionally, they were supposed to be firewood gatherers, cooks, herb doctors, builders, and healers. The Hopi and Navajo have dozens of clans and sub-clans, including Bear Strap Clan.

Significantly, the word for clan in Cherokee is simply a collective or plural prefix meaning "animate beings" or "people" (*ani*). The Seven Clans are called in Cherokee *gatligwogi itsuniyvwi*, literally "seven types of creatures," the latter word being related to the tribal name of the Cherokee Ani-Yunwiya (Principal People). Anthropologists like James Mooney, Albert S. Gatschet, and Herman J. Viola termed these social units *gentes*, the Latin word for "people," a word that conveys the idea of nationalities or ethnicities. They are not clans in the customary sense of the word. It can't be imagined that a Cherokee of a certain "clan" could easily find "courtesy kinship" with other clan members while traveling among other tribes. Cherokee and other clan systems were to some degree incompatible. So let us give a brief description of each.

Wolf Clan. This is perhaps the oldest clan and by far the most numerous today. They are also called the Dohdewah, elders, teachers, people to carry on beliefs and traditions. Wolftown on the Eastern Cherokee Reservation in North Carolina is named after it, and there are Cherokees with the surname Wolf or Wolfe, especially in North Carolina. Its foundation goes back to the beginning of the Ani-Yunwiya, or Principal People.

4

Here is the Cherokee-origin story as I heard it from a Tennessee elder in the 1990s.

Story of the Sacred Dog

When the pioneers came through the Cumberland Gap into Tennessee they stumbled onto the Cherokee stronghold. They followed what was known as the Avery Trace. On its northern end, this went to Kentucky and joined the Great Warrior Path to Iroquois lands. On its southern end, it continued on through Nashville and became the Natchez Trace. These roads once connected empires. They went from capital to capital, sacred place to sacred place. The Cherokee had their sacred place on Monterey Mountain. It was marked by a stone monument to their national hero, the dog. The people had carved a large dog out of the top of the mountain in gratitude for their deliverance in the long-ago times.

Before the Great Flood there lived a man and his wife in a land now below the waters called Lami. There were no Cherokee at that time. The people of that place were a single nation with one tongue.

Many had become wicked. They turned to witchcraft to satisfy their desires. This man and his wife kept to the old ways and were faithful. They had a dog that was loyal to them, that they loved very much.

The dog spoke to the man and his wife in their dreams. One night it told them the world was going to be destroyed. They should make preparations to save their family. The man did not want to believe this. When he saw the dog in the morning he asked the animal what he meant. The dog whimpered and cowered and tried to show fear. The man shook his head. He petted the dog but the dog was not to be comforted. Finally, the dog took the man down to the river and jumped into the rushing water. To show the man what he meant, he tore his arm and leg muscles with his teeth and drowned. The dog gave his life to save the lives of his people.

The man now knew what he was to do. He began building a boat. He put food and other necessities on it. The neighbors laughed at him because the ocean was far away even though they lived on an island. The stream was too small to carry his boat. When the man tried to warn them, they made fun of him for talking with dogs! It began to rain, and they ridiculed him all the more. The man quietly gathered his family and loaded their things on the boat.

The flood waters swept them down the river to the sea. It rained for many months. There were earthquakes and the entire earth was covered with water. Finally, their boat came to rest on Monterey Mountain [in Putnam County, Tennessee]. This is why the Cherokee still live in the mountains, because they are afraid of another flood. They do not like to live where there are no cedar trees either.

The man and his wife had children, and the children had children. The Cherokees spread out to the east and settled the Cherokee outlet to the sea along the Savannah River. They are called the Principal People [*ani yunwiya*] to show they are all descended from this couple. The original Wolf Clan is still the most common.

What happened to the Dog? The settlers in the Cumberland chipped away at it. Soldiers dynamited it. The atrocious Bledsoe brothers built their fort in the middle of the Avery Trace overlooking sacred ceremony ground. They took potshots at the Indians who came to trade and worship there. By the end of the century after they had left the region, the Cherokee Dog had dwindled to a foreleg. This was removed by some civic group. Eventually, it was placed on a pedestal in a park in the nearby town of Monterey, where you can see it today, although the fragment is not recognizable as part of a dog.

The Wolf Clan is related to, but not the same as, the Warrior Society of the Cherokee, the Shalokee or Eshelokee (with a soft *sh*, as distinct from the tribal name Tsalagi or Cherokee), a word that means "volunteer settlers" in the Greek language. Clan members excelled supposedly at warfare and were noted for their fierce loyalty and protection of family. A famous Wolf Clan matriarch was Nancy Moytoy, daughter of Quatsi (Patsy) of Tellico, who named one of her sons Big Dog, another White Dog, and was the mother of Tame Doe, whose daughter by the Arabicized Englishman Francis Ward (Wardiyah, "the Rose") was Nancy Ward, the Beloved or War Woman, also called the Cherokee Rose (d. 1824). Nancy Moytoy adopted Attakullakulla, an Algonquian boy, into the Wolf Clan. Nancy's two brothers, Motoy II and Old Hop, were chiefs, and it was she who adopted the British agent John Stuart into the Wolf Clan. Charles Hicks was another chief from the Wolf Clan.

In the Cherokee DNA study at DNA Consultants, an enrolled member of the Cherokee Nation of Oklahoma, Gayl A. Wilson (born Gibson) traced her Wolf Clan line to Sarah Consene, a daughter of Young Dragging Canoe whose mother was in the same line as Nancy Ward and Nancy Moytoy. The mitochondrial lineage is C, one of the four classic American Indian haplogroups that crossed into North America from Siberia and Mongolia. Her particular haplotype appears to be widespread, matching dozens of Hispanic Americans and Mexicans.

The Algonquian Indians also have a Wolf Clan, and the Cherokees' claim to be called the Dog People may have something to do with the Chichimeca (Dog Lineage) tribes of Mexico, associated with the barbarian north and remembered as predecessor peoples to the civilized Toltecs and Teotihuacanos who came later. Chichimeca in turn may be related to Chickamauga, the militant faction of the Cherokee at the end of their existence as a sovereign entity.

Artist's conception of original eight-foot-tall sandstone Sacred Dog near Monterey, Tenn. It stood guard over the homeland of the Cherokees on the Avery Trace, facing westward in the direction they originated from. *Dillard.*

Standing Stone monument in Monterey
park today with Phyllis Starnes, Paint Clan
descendant. *Billy Starnes.*

The color of the Wolf was red, which also stood for war and all things sacred or beloved.

Bird Clan. This has been compared to the Delaware Indians' Turkey Clan, Thunderbird and Eagle Clan of certain tribes and is the second most common among the Cherokee. It is an important division among the Hopi, Zuni and Pueblo Indians, as well. Together with the Wolf, Bear and Deer, it was probably one of the core clans of the Ani-Yunwiyah or Principal People. To credit the most authoritative materials (Bettis), the original name of this clan was Red Flicker, Sapsucker, Woodpecker or Ani-Tsaliena or Tsunilyana, meaning Deaf Clan. Both the Wolf and Deer clans were derived from it. There are many reasons to associate it with Mexico and Central America. According to several accounts, the Cherokee migrated from the south, becoming the first of the Southeastern Tribes to travel north and cross the Mississippi, settling after a circuitous route in the lower Appalachian Mountains. Birdtown in North Carolina is a stronghold, though there are more Wolf

Clan members than Bird Clan there. Note that just because your last name is Bird (as in the former chief of the Cherokee Nation of Oklahoma, Joe Byrd) does not mean you are Bird Clan, since patrilineal surnames have replaced the traditional clan system. Many chiefs, particularly peace chiefs, are Thunderbird Clan, a sort of honorary sub-clan of Bird.

Outline of 180-foot-long quartzite Rock Eagle Mound, a shingle-covered earthwork of a thunderbird that probably marked a chief's grave from more than 2,000 years ago, in Putnam County, Ga. The mound is egg-shaped. *Google Satellite.*

Rock Eagle panoramic view. *Rock Eagle 4-H Center, Eatonton, Ga.*

Bird Clan members were, by custom, messengers. They made excellent speakers, heralds and news bearers. Typically, a Speaker (Skalilosken) sat or stood on the principal chief's left-hand side in ceremonial situations and in the council house; the war chief was to his right. If a stranger or foreigner approached the village, a herald, often an elder of the Bird Clan, would be sent to meet him.

It was a sin for anyone to kill a wolf since wolves (warriors) protected the people, but it was also a sin for Bird Clan members to hunt a bird since they would become guilty of murder and fratricide. The same could be said of deer meat and Deer Clan. Nevertheless, clan members could eat the meat of a clan totem killed by someone else. Only Bird Clan members were allowed to catch eagles and harvest their feathers.

Alexander Sanders, one of the assassins of Doublehead, was Bird Clan through his mother Susannah, wife of Mitchell Sanders, and Doublehead was Paint Clan – by which we can glimpse the inter-clan machinery of revenge. Chief John Ross (1790-1866) was Bird Clan, descended in the strict female line from Ghi-goo-ie (Ghigau, Beloved or War Woman), wife of William Shorey, a Scotsman and likely crypto-Jew whose surname was Hebrew ("bull," a name used for Joseph). His boyhood name was Cooweescoowee, a rare water-bird that only infrequently visited the Cherokee homeland, later the name of a judicial district in Indian Territory. Quatie Conrad was also Bird Clan. She married Alexander Brown, Archibald Fields and John Benge.

Deer Clan is the third of the original clans. Deer Clan members are supposed to be good runners, ball players, clothes makers, tanners and intellects. Anawaika or Deerhead Cove at the foot of Fox Mountain between northern Georgia and Alabama, near Lookout Mountain, was a traditional territory of the Deer Clan. Part of Paint-town in North Carolina was once called Deer Place.

Nancy Ward's first husband, Kingfisher, was Deer Clan. Major John Ridge (The Ridge) and Oowatie or David Watie were brothers, the children of Oconostota or Tatchee (Dutch), of the Paint Clan, and a woman of the Deer Clan,

16

so they were both Deer. Major Ridge married Susannah Wickett of the Wild Potato Clan, and David Watie married Susannah Reece, daughter of Nancy Adair. David and Susannah's children included Buck Watie (who adopted the name Elias Boudinot, and who married Harriet Gold, a New Englander) and Gen. Elias (Stand) Watie, who had wives from the Fields, Miller, Looney and Bell families.

Deer Clan women sometimes adopted fawns, suckling and raising them as pets. Nancy Ward's mother was Tame Doe, whose name indicates there was Deer Clan in her lines. Note that you never receive a name that echoes your mother's clan. Thus, Attakullakulla's original Nippising clan was Bear before he was adopted by Nancy Moytoy (Wolf) and her husband, an Algonquian Indian of unknown clan, and his boyhood name was White Owl. He is depicted with a pet bear in the Trustees of Georgia painting. He received the name Attakullakulla (Little Carpenter) later in life in tribute to his statecraft and treaty making.

Attakullakulla married women of different clans and named one of their sons Little White Owl. This was also the name of one of Dragging Canoe's sons. Hence, we can see that some names were handed down in the male line among the Cherokee. This tendency to use patronymics was enhanced after the abolishment of the clan laws. For instance, Young Dragging Canoe (Paint) married Nancy Hughes (Wolf) and all their children received the surname Consene or Connesuna (Canoe).

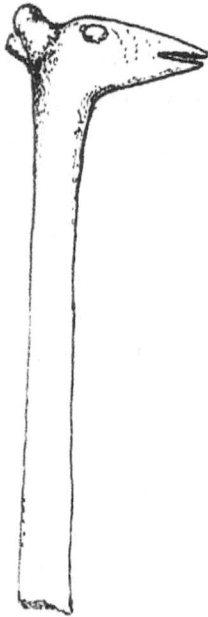

Bone doe-head pin from about 700-950 CE. Deer Woman was the keeper of animals and gardens. She was the patroness of childbirth, love, fertility, plenitude and all the arts. *Diaz-Granados and Duncan.*

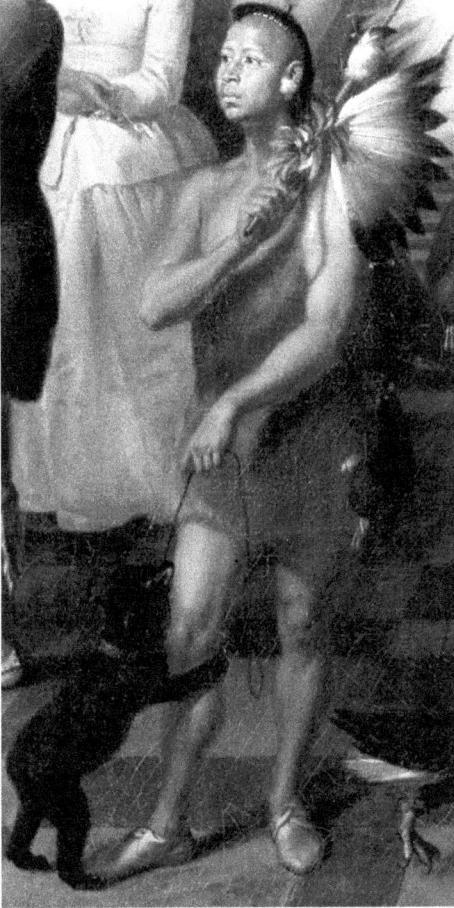

White Owl (Attakullakulla) with bear mascot and eagle feathers in Cherokee delegation to King George II, 1730. *Winterthur Museum.*

Twister Clan. Also known as Long Hair or Wind or Twisted Hair. There are a lot of false notions about the Twister Clan, Cherokee Ani-Kiloki, or Hilohi, or Gilogi. This name means "people from Gilo" and can be taken as strictly Hawaiian. Gi-lolo was the land where the earliest ancestors of the Hawaiians came from, identified by later Spanish, Dutch and English navigators as the Moluccas in the Indonesian Archipelago. According to Keetoowah traditions, the original Cherokee arrived in America with "a bunch of Polynesians they brought with them." In Hawaiian, Hilo means "braid, twisted" (compare Greek *illa,* "rope"; *hilo,* "twist, wrap"; *hilex,* "twisting"). The legend goes that Hawaii's capital city Hilo got its name from the natives' skill in twisting together plant fibers to make rope. The same root appears in hula, the dance ("twist"). Such a derivation explains why the Twister clan members "were once a proud people who strutted when they walked and twisted their shoulders in a haughty manner." The Anigilohi clan's cultural memory evidently reflects its ancient connection with the Polynesians who accompanied the Eshelokee – the People from Hilo. Such identification may also explain why Twisters were considered by the other clans as extraneous foreigners, a group composed of prisoners of war, captives and refugees who had only a tenuous connection to the Cherokee. Tagwadihi, a Cherokee medicine man photographed by James Mooney in the 1890s (see illustration this page), not only physically resembles Native Hawaiians but also seems to bear a Hawaiian name, one that may be derived from the Greek. The word *dakwa* means whale or sea monster in Greek. Anthropologists note that the word was also used of the Cherokee's enemies, the Cawtabas. They usually translate the medicine man's name as Catawba Killer. But Takea is the name of the shark in Hawaiian folklore, and Shark Killer and the like are common Hawaiian surnames. In legend, Maui's sister is

21

repeatedly helped by Takea and other sharks. It was a common rite of passage for Polynesian boys to kill a shark. Probably the Catawbas are called *tagwa* simply because Catawba, which is Siouan, reminded the Cherokee of a word in their own language, much as an Englishman might call a Frank or Frenchman a "Frog." Curiously, one of Maui's names is Talaga, very close to Tsalagi. Maui's father was Tangaroa or Tanoa (seemingly designating a Danaan or Greek). Tanoa was the father of all fair-haired children and came from a land called Atia.

Atia, which appears to be the same word as Attica, was the ancient Polynesian homeland to the West, full of high alabaster temples. One of them

> ...was very spacious, and was built as a meeting-place for gods and men; and here after death the spirits of the ancients foregathered with the gods. Here originated different kinds of sports, and games and feasts to the gods Rongo', Tane', Rua-nuku, Tu', Tangaroa, and Tongaiti. Here were meeting-places for the great chiefs of those days . . . when appointing

rulers, and devising measures for the good of the people. Here, too, originated the wars that caused the people to enter and spread over the Pacific.

One could hardly invent a more fitting folk memory of Greek culture. Athens, the capital of Attica, was the envy of the world for its marble buildings dedicated to the gods of Olympus, its trade, games, amusements, learning, food, luxuries, art, philosophy, military prowess and democratic government. It is estimated that the ancestors of the Polynesians left this land when it was governed by the great king Tu-te-rangi-marama about 450 BCE, a date that corresponds exactly with Athens' golden age under Pericles. The Hawaiian word that epitomized this lost world is *karioi*, "leisure, ease," literally the same word in Greek for "amusements." Christian missionaries fought to eradicate Polynesians' pursuit of *karioi*, often translating the beloved concept in English as "lewdness."

Traditions also say the Twisters or Stranger Clan were the priests, teachers and keepers of ancient lore. William

Eubanks (Cornsilk), a Keetoowah priest, wrote that the Cherokee identity, or their true name, "has never been found out, and perhaps never will be," but it is a designation given to those "initiated as a tribe into the eastern mysteries . . . by a wise branch of the tribe known as those who spoke the language of Seg." Seg is an Austronesian language of Indonesia, part of the very large language family known as Central-Eastern-Malayo Polynesian, with a western form called Thai-Seg and eastern form spoken in the Madang province of Papua New Guinea known as Sek, or Gedaged. The word points to dispersals from Sundaland and initial sea voyages of the Melanesians and Polynesians since it is the name of an important non-native clan in New Guinea.

The Pale Prophet of the Hawaiians as well as their Cherokee counterparts was the white demigod Maui ("guide, navigator" in Egyptian) of the Far West, who introduced all civilized arts and crafts and "fished islands from the deep." He lent the Cherokee their title for principal chief, Amatoyhi or Moytoy "mariner, admiral." Historically, he probably

24

corresponds to the Libyan leader of a fleet dispatched by the pharaoh Ptolemy III to set the international dateline and circumnavigate the world after it was proved to be round by Eratosthenes, director of the Library at Alexandria, in the years before 230 BCE. Records of these voyages are extant in cave drawings at Sosorra on the northwest coast of New Guinea and an inscription in a cave near Santiago, Chile and seem to be reflected in Hopi traditions.

Haplogroup B (and to a lesser extent C) is characteristic of Twister Clan descendants. For instance, a direct maternal-line descendant of Lucretia Parris, half blood daughter of George Parris and granddaughter of early Cherokee Indian trader Richard Pearis (died in the Bahamas, April 7, 1794) is haplogroup B. Pearis married a Twister Clan woman. Another Twister Clan descendant is Elvis Presley, through his mother Gladys Love, going back in an unbroken female line to Nancy Burdine, a Jewess of Kentucky, whose mother was a Cherokee woman named White Dove. Presley's mitochondrial haplotype is B.

Another famous Twister was Elizabeth Tassel, one of the first Cherokee women to wed an English frontier official, Scottish trader Ludovic Grant, about 1726. The marriage bore only one daughter, Mary Grant, who in turn wed William Emory, another trader, but it was prolific in later generations, producing many celebrated Cherokee names: Due, Watts, Corntassel, Stuart, Rogers and Waters. Oklahoma cowboy humorist and author Will Rogers (1879-1935) is among them. Samuel Riley, one of the founders of Northeast Alabama, married two sisters, Gulustiyu and Nigodigeyu, of the Twister Clan.

Emergence petroglyphs in Hawaii (left) and at Burnt Ridge Petroglyph Site, Madison County, Kentucky are similar in style and meaning. All celebrate the Sea Peoples who came from the West. Their founding mother figure was called Pretty Woman or Friendly Woman, another name for the Twister Clan (in Cherokee, Ulilahi). *DNA Consultants Blog.*

House built in 1804 by Joseph Vann, a Wild Potato Clan member, in northern Georgia is a showcase today. It was one of the first Cherokee dwellings to be confiscated by the Georgia Guard in Indian Removal in 1838. *Chief Vann House Historic Site.*

Wild Potato Clan. The Ani-Kotakewe, or Gotagewe, or Gotegewi are related to the Twisters by their migrations or origins in foreign lands. Both are clans that joined the original three, the Bird, Wolf and Deer. Also known as Blind Savannah, Long Prairie, Acorn and Walnut, Wild Potato Clan members were keepers of religious customs, writings and games.

It seems that the Ani-Gotegewi, or Wild Potato Clan, just like the Twister Clan, exist only among the Cherokee. This clan seems to reflect the Cherokees' travels in South America. Potatoes come from Peru and were not grown in North America until their introduction by Europeans. Could it be that the name of this clan in the singular, Gotegewa, pronounced approximately K'tigwa, is a corruption of Quechua, the original name of the Andean people we know today as the Incas? Others attempt to derive the name from Kituwah, or Keetoowah, but the question may be moot, since the names Quechua and Kituwah appear to come from the same Semitic language, ancient Egyptian. Both the Keetoowah Society,

Scribal Society and Wild Potato Clan, then, appear to be connected to Greek, Jewish, Phoenician and Egyptian culture.

Keetoowah priests speak of travels through the Sacred Lakes in South America, for according to tradition, the Cherokee once allowed their Sacred Fire, the eternal flame maintained in the national heptagon, called *catahyis* (Greek for "assembly house"), to go out. They had to send a delegation of Keetoowah priests to South America to bring a new one from the source. Could this have been at the famed Valley of the Immortals in south Ecuador? This ancient site is renowned for its seven craterlike lakes, sources for streams that flow into the Inca pilgrimage city of Vilcabamba (Quechua for "Sacred Valley"). The area is now a national park. Its unique mineral waters are reputed to be so healthful that many residents live to be over a hundred.

Alexander Dougherty, a Jacobite fleeing Ireland to Virginia, was the first white man to marry a Cherokee, in 1690. We do not know her clan. After 1719, Cornelius Dougherty, his son, became a trader out of Charleston in Keowee in

Lower Cherokee Country and married Ah-nee-wa-kee, a daughter of Chief Moytoy II (Amadohiyi), thus fulfilling the usual contract. She was of the Wild Potato Clan. Another Wild Potato Clan matriarch was Susannah or Sonicooie, who married Thomas Cordery. Their descendants included Sarah Cordery who married John Rogers and many enrolled Cherokees by the names Vickery, Harris, McNair, Mosley and Collins. The Nighthawk Society of Redbird Smith emphasized genealogies and traditions of the Wild Potato. James Vann and Sour Mash were Wild Potato. So was Sickatower, one of the oldest men in the nation around 1800, when he became a source for ethnographic notes on the Cherokee.

Panther (or Blue Paint) Clan. By all accounts, this clan is almost extinct. Its members were also known as "Dangerous Men" and "Night People." Other minor clans seem to be collapsed within it, such as Bear Clan, Tiger Clan, Wildcat Clan and Raccoon Clan. Its Cherokee name is Ani-Sahoni or Sakanike ("purple"), which means "They sit in the ashes until they turn blue-gray." Because West African medicine men are distinguished by white or blue face paint created from ashes, this could represent the African component in the Cherokee melting pot. Tribal traditions emphasize that the Cherokee include black people as well as white, red, and yellow. I have been unable to find any representative genealogies. It may be said to be the least known of the clans.

Hastings Shade told Brian Wilkes the true name is Sahoni, the ancient word for the saber-tooth lion, used now for any large cat, and as in the calendric day-sign Panther, which in the north replaces the Mayan-Aztec jaguar sign. Both cats would be called *sahoni* in Cherokee. The same word is used for the medicine plant known as blue holly and blind savannah, somehow related to the big cat. By holly is meant *Ilex vomitaria*, yaupon or cassena, the herb used in the ceremonial "white drink" (or "black drink") of the oldest Indians of the southwestern U.S., including the Creeks, Miccosukee, Appalachee, Yuchi, Calusa, Timucua, Yamasee, Guale and Tihanama. Another name is Ani-Seluyahi (Blue Corn). The Hopi are also known as the Blue Corn People. The Hopi call the

Cherokee the White Corn People and Elder Brother. According to Keetoowah Society elders, the Cherokee once spoke a non-Indian language akin to Hopi, but gave it up and adopted Mohawk to continue to live with the Iroquois. The "old tongue" seems to have many elements of Greek, the language of Ptolemaic Egypt and ancient Judeans.

Paint Clan. We have saved the Ani-Wodi for last, referred to both as red and blue paint people, the former being much more common, the latter being, as we have seen above with the Panther Clan, almost extinct. According to John Payne's informants about 1820, the Paint Clan was the most numerous, not Wolf. Paint People seems, without question, to be the ordinary name for Phoenicians, whose name for themselves was *Knai* "Canaanites," rendered in Native America as Kanawa, the name of a river, and Conoy Indians, mentioned by Adair as a Canaanite tribe. Phoinikoi, the Greek term, was used to designate people associated with phoenix, a mythological bird that rose from its own ashes, the date palm and a reddish-blue or purple dye, all

emblems of Phoenician or Punic
civilization. Phoenician trade was founded
on Tyrian purple, a violet-purple dye
derived from the Murex sea-snail's shell.
They also stepped into the copper and tin

Paint Clan necklace with severely crimped
Phoenician copper coin dating from before
141 BCE showing goddess of the sea
Tanith and dolphins on obverse and horse
and palm trees on reverse. *Donald Yates.*

trade of the Minoans after about 1200 BCE, moving their center of operations successively from Lebanon to Asia Minor to Carthage. After the Third Punic War, the Phoenician state was defeated and dissolved by Rome.

By tradition, Paint Clan members were the doctors and hunters (*kanati*, from Greek *gennadi* "noblemen"), keepers of history (*tikano*, from Greek *tynchana* "events") and prophecy, and masters of protocol, diplomacy and ceremony. Peace chiefs and Ukus ("owls," or wise men, in the Greek model; cf. Hopi *mongwi* "owl, chief") were often chosen from Paint Clan ranks.

The Paint Clan was never called anything but by its true name, Paint (*wodi*). No other clans were combined with it. One of its privileges was mask making, a sign of its origins in the ancient Mediterranean (see cover). Another was music and song. Paint Clan people were also adept at the magical arts. All these characteristics are summed up in the figure of Stoneclad, or Stonecoat. He is a fierce warlock responsible for bestowing on the Cherokees specific medicinal formulas and knowledge, hunting songs, the *urim* and *thummim* crystals [*ulungstata*, cf. Greek *ouluntata* "judged healthy"] used for divining, and the red clay used for face and body painting. He is called an *askili* or *tsasgili/tchaskili*, "witch," which can also mean owl.

When Stoneclad dies he is given a funeral pyre. He sings forth all of his magical charms and storied knowledge for everyone to hear and bequeaths to the seven clans a firm foundation for the Cherokee Nation. Henceforth it is taboo for any Cherokee to add to the stories and songs of old. He is thus a culture-hero.

According to musicologists, Cherokee music is unusual for its so-called anhemitonic scales, music with only four, five or six pitches, a characteristic also of ancient Greek music. It is found in the stomp dance, peculiar to the Cherokee. Cherokee music is noteworthy in featuring water drums, flutes and leg rattles, instruments with a deep history in Egypt.

Unlike other clans, Paint Clan members could, and were almost expected to, marry with other Paint Clan members, often a cousin. When cousin-marriage occurred, Paint Clan affinity was handed down in the male line as well as the female. Some of them practiced Judaism, although United Keetoowah elders vehemently deny this. Others say Judaism was also found in the Deer Clan.

In Phase I and II of "Anomalous Cherokee Mitochondrial DNA Lineages," many Paint Clan descendants proved to be haplogroup $U2e^*$ or X. One of the cases of $U2e^*$ is my own, an anomalous Cherokee type also found in other study participants and traced to Libya and Greece in ancient times. This line evidently arose from a Jewish Indian trader and a Cherokee woman. My fifth-great-grandmother was born about 1790 on the northern Georgia and southwestern North Carolina frontier and had a relationship with a trader named Enoch Jordan. The trader's male line descendants from his white family in North Carolina possess Y chromosomal J, a common Jewish type. Some Jordans, in fact, bear the Cohen

Modal Haplotype or genetic signature of Old Testament Priests. My mother, Bessie Cooper, was a double descendant of Cherokee chief Black Fox (d. 1811, Paint Clan) and was born on Sand Mountain in northeastern Alabama near Black Fox's former seat at Creek Path.

Four generations of mitochondrial haplogroup U2 with Libyan woman. From left: Mary Nell Anderson, author's sister; our mother Bessie C. Yates; her mother Dovie Palestine Cooper; the latter's maternal aunt Mary Lackey Haston; and a woman from Cyrenaica about 1930. Mary Lackey's great- grandmother was the Cherokee woman who married Trader Jordan. *Family photos; Alinari.*

Nancy Ward statue attributed to James Abraham Walker. The Beloved Woman is shown holding a blackfox (not lamb—lambs don't have long tails) symbolic of the new state of Watauga which she protected. The statue was stolen in the 1970s, placed on a white woman's grave in another cemetery, lost again, sold to an antiques dealer in New England, but is in process of being recovered and restored as a Tennessee historical monument at last report. ©*David Ray Smith. Used by permission.*

Ancient terracotta mask from Carthage. This grotesque type, which flourished for centuries in the Punic west, probably inspired the Cherokees' and Iroquois' booger dance masks. Just as the Phoenicians specialized in decorative mask manufacture and distribution in antiquity, the Paint Clan held a monopoly on mask making among the Cherokee. *Markoe.*

Dockyards of Carthage at the height of Phoenician sea power could hold over a thousand ships, most of them merchantmen, including 220 warships. Fell estimated the total number of crewmen serving on Phoenician ships in 261 BCE to be 150,000. *Norwich.*

Just as the Paint Clan served as the foundation and tutor for the Seven Clans, its leaders forged a new type of government following the disasters of the Revolutionary War, when the Cherokee were allied with the British. Earlier, the Echota chiefs had began to deliver written copies of their "talks," a practice unparalleled in any other Indian tribe. These expanded versions developed a notion of justice and just

40

relations, and they acted as a durable record for arguments that might otherwise be swept away. Oconostota (Paint Clan) even wrote letters to the editor of the Knoxville Gazette published after his death in 1792. Gradually, the Cherokee were able to send embassies to Washington, hire lawyers and accountants there and retain lobbyists for their cause. New Echota in northern Georgia became the fledgling new capital, with an official newspaper called the Cherokee Phoenix. Like that uncanny symbol of Phoenicians constantly reinventing themselves, the Cherokee republic rose from the ashes of the old.

Blackfox from nineteenth century cigarette card. *New York Public Library.*

References

Andersen, Johannes C. (1986). *Myths and Legends of the Polynesians.* Rutland: Tuttle.

Bettis, R. Mack. Notes on six Cherokee gentes [card files in the Smithsonian Institution], by Albert S. Gatschet, including notations by James Mooney and J.N.B. Hewitt recording information from Cherokee medicine man John Ax among others, together with manuscript materials by J.T. Garrett, interpreted by John D. Strange, Allogan Slagle and Mack Bettis, and kindly shared with the author by the last named. Also to be thanked is Herman Viola, director of the Smithsonian's Anthropological Archives, who facilitated access of these materials in 1974.

Cherokee Nation of Oklahoma Cultural Resource Center, P.O. Box 948, Tahlequah, OK 74465.

Cox, Brent Yanusdi (1999). *Heart of the Eagle.* Milan: Chenanee.

Eubanks, William (Cornsilk, ca. 1900). "Cherokee Legend of the Son of Man. The Red Race, It is Claimed by this Writer, Were the Originators of the Ancient Apollo Worship, Now Known as the Christian Religion," in *A Collection of Works by William Eubanks*, ed. Doug Weatherly and Kristy Hales. American Native Press Archives and Sequoyah Research Center. Published online: http://www.anpa.ualr.edu/digital_library/WehEuba.html.

Fell, Barry (1980). *Saga America*. New York: Times. See esp. "The Great Navigations," pp. 262-95.

Gilbert, William Harlan (1925). "Eastern Cherokee Social Organization," in *Social Anthropology of Eastern American Indian Tribes*, ed. Fred Eggan. Chicago: Open Library.

Hecht, Marjorie Mazel (1998). "The Decipherment and Discovery of a Voyage to America in 232 B.C.," *21st Century Science & Technology* 1998/1999:62-65.

Herm, Gerhard (1975). *The Phoenicians. The Purple Empire of the Ancient World.* New York: Morrow.

Mails, Thomas E. (1992). *The Cherokee People.* Tulsa: Council Oaks.

Meredith, Howard L. and Virginia E. Milan, ed. (n.d.). *Cherokee Vision of Eloh',* trans. Wesley Proctor. Muskogee: Indian UP. Orig. pub. in *Indian Chieftain,* 1896.

Panther-Yates, Donald N. (2001). "A Portrait of Cherokee Chief Attakullakulla from the 1730s? A Discussion of William Verelst's 'Trustees of Georgia' Painting'," *Journal of Cherokee Studies* 22:4-20.

------------------ (2001). "Cherokee Story of the Sacred Dog of Monterey Mountain And the Great Flood: A Comparison of the Living Story with Mooney's Version," paper delivered at panel on "Storytelling and Contemporary Native American Culture," at the Southern States Communication Association National Conference Lexington, Ky., April 8, 2001.

Payne, John Howard (1832-38). Papers on the Cherokee (MSS and typescripts available on DVD). Newberry Library, Chicago, Ayer MS 698.

Starr, Emmet (1921). *History of the Cherokee Indians.* Oklahoma City: Warden.

Strickland, Rennard (1975). *Fire and the Spirits. Cherokee Law from Clan to Court.* Norman: U of Oklahoma P.

Wilkes, Brian. Personal communications. 11 November 2005 *et seq.*

Yates, Donald N. (2010). "Anomalous Mitochondrial DNA Lineages in the Cherokee." *Ancient American* 14/86:28-32.

Cherokee Chapbooks

Other Titles in the Cherokee Chapbooks Series

Red Man's Origin, as Told by Sahkiya Sanders

A Memoir of Chief Two White Feathers

Echo the Heart: The Tihanama Language

www.ingramcontent.com/pod-product-compliance
Lightning Source LLC
Chambersburg PA
CBHW060623030426
42337CB00018B/3161